Healthy Homemade

Cat Food

Enjoy Preparing this Collection of Cat Food Recipes that Are Sure to Leave Your Furry Friend Purring with Delight!

BY

Rachael Rayner

License Notes

Indigo

our refund policy

Refunds or exchanges may be made within 30 days if item is returned in store-bought condition with a receipt, unless subject to our great read guarantee which item(s) may be returned and exchanged at any time and in any condition, with a receipt. Items with a gift receipt may be exchanged or refunded onto a gift card for the value of the item at the time of purchase. See indigo.ca for full return policy.

enjoy our best deals with plum® PLUS.
not a member? join today for $39/year.

enjoy these member benefits in-store and online:

- save 10% on almost everything!*
- enjoy free shipping every day*
- earn 5 plum points on almost every dollar spent*
- celebrate your birthday with 20% off*

541913927

Pickup Date/Time : **Mon, 19 Jan 2026 11:00 PM**

Krystyna MacDuff

Table of Contents

Introduction

This book will give you an easy-to-follow introduction into the world of homemade cat food. The collection of recipes are not complicated, so before you know it, you will be whipping them up for your furry friend in no time at all. When you make your own cat food, it allows you to be in total control of exactly what you are feeding your beloved pet. You are going to be in control of what is included in your cat's diet as you will be the one preparing it from start to finish. No more trying to guess whether the food has the proper healthy ingredients in it—you can add all the healthy ingredients yourself.

By learning exactly what your cat's nutritional needs are you can then decide what homemade cat food will suit their personal needs. You have a great selection of homemade cat foods and treats that you can choose from to prepare for your beloved cat. It will also make you feel good in knowing exactly what your pet's food contains in it—making sure that you are feeding them a healthy diet will make you think that you are providing them with the best nutrition for them to thrive!

Chapter 1. Cooked Homemade Cat Food Recipes

Turkey and Pasta Cat Meal

Here is a homemade cat food recipe for that furry friend that has a love for turkey!

Preparation time: 10 minutes

Total Cooking time: 20 minutes

Servings: 4 cups

Ingredients:

- 100 mg taurine supplement
- ½ teaspoon bone meal
- 1 teaspoon dried parsley
- ½ cup plain nonfat Greek yogurt
- 2 large egg whites, beaten
- 1 cup whole-grain elbow pasta
- 1 pound lean ground turkey breast

Directions:

1. Cook your turkey in a skillet over medium-high heat for about 10 minutes or until browned, then drain extra grease from the pan.

2. Bring a pot of salted water to a boil, then add in the pasta and cook to al dente, for about 10 minutes.

3. Drain the pasta and set it aside.

4. Add the turkey to your food processor, then reheat the skillet and cook the egg whites until set.

5. Add the cooked egg and pasta into the food processor along with yogurt, bone meal, parsley, and taurine.

6. Pulse the cat food mixture until well combined but not entirely pureed.

7. Cool the mixture before serving to your pet.

Sardine & Chicken Liver Dinner

This is a dinner recipe that is sure to become one of your cat's favorites that they will come running to enjoy!

Preparation time: 10 minutes

Total Cooking time: 45 minutes

Servings: 6

Ingredients:

- 100 mg taurine supplement
- 1 cup cooked red lentils, drained
- 1 ½ cups white rice, steamed
- 1 ½ pounds whole roaster chicken, skin removed

Directions:

1. Chop the chicken and place it into your stockpot and cover with water and bring to a boil over medium-high heat.

2. Reduce heat of pot, then simmer the chicken until it is cooked through for about 45 minutes. Drain and shred the chicken meat.

3. Add your chicken to your food processor along with cooked rice and lentils.

4. Pulse the cat food mixture about several times then add in the taurine supplement.

5. Allow your cat food mixture to cool before serving to your cat.

Creamy Salmon Pasta Dish

For that furry friend that you know has a special love for salmon then this might be the perfect homemade cat food to prepare for them.

Preparation time: 10 minutes

Total Cooking time: 55 minutes

Servings: 6

Ingredients:

- 100 mg taurine supplement
- 4 tablespoons kelp powder
- ¼ cup shredded cheddar cheese
- ¼ cup frozen spinach, thawed and drained
- 1 cup whole-grain elbow pasta
- 1 pound salmon fillet, boneless (skin okay)

Directions:

1. Brush your salmon fillet with some olive oil and broil in the oven until it is just cooked through for about 45 minutes.

2. Cook the pasta in a pot with some lightly salted water, enough to cover the pasta, cook your dish until al dente, for about 10 minutes then drain.

3. Combine your cooked pasta with the cheese, spinach, kelp powder, and taurine in a food processor.

4. Add the salmon to the food processor by flaking it.

5. Pulse the salmon mixture about several times or until it is thoroughly combined.

6. Cool the salmon mixture before serving to your cat.

Beefy Potato Casserole

This kitty casserole will be a real treat for your kitty cat that they will not want to miss!

Preparation time: 10 minutes

Total Cooking time: 45 minutes

Servings: 6

Ingredients:

- ¼ cup unsweetened almond milk
- 2 to 3 tablespoons grated Parmesan cheese
- ½ cup cottage cheese, pureed
- 3 cups parboiled potatoes, peeled and sliced thin
- 100 mg taurine supplement
- 1/8 teaspoon psyllium husk powder
- ½ teaspoon powdered calcium supplement
- 1 teaspoon brewers yeast
- 1 pound lean ground beef

Directions:

1. Preheat your oven to 350° Fahrenheit. Lightly grease your casserole dish with some cooking spray.

2. Cook the ground beef for about half an hour in the oven or until it is browned, then drain fat.

3. Stir in the brewers' yeast along with psyllium husk powder, taurine supplement, and calcium.

4. Spread the ground beef mixture in the bottom of the casserole dish.

5. Place potato slices over the beef and sprinkle with cottage cheese and Parmesan.

6. Pour milk over mixture then bake for another 15 minutes or until the cheese has melted.

7. Remove the cat casserole from oven and allow it to cool before serving to your pet.

Cornish Hen Dish

This is a dish that your feline friend will enjoy full-heartedly from start to finish!

Preparation time: 10 minutes

Full Cook time: 25 minutes

Servings: 6-8

Ingredients:

- 50 mg taurine supplement
- 2 tablespoons bone meal
- 2 tablespoons kelp powder
- ¼ cup mashed sweet potato
- 2 large egg whites, beaten
- 1 pound fresh Cornish game hen meat, chopped
- 1 tablespoon olive oil
- 2 cups old-fashioned oats

Directions:

1. Cook your oats according to the package directions, then set aside to cool.

2. Heat the oil in a pan over medium-high heat.

3. Add the Cornish game hen meat and cook the meat for about 15 minutes or until browned, stirring often.

4. Remove the chicken from pan and place it in a mixing bowl. Reheat the skillet using the cooking grease from the game meat.

5. Add the egg whites to pan and scramble until they are cooked through.

6. Add the game hen meat back into the pan along with mashed sweet potato, bone meal, kelp powder, and taurine supplement.

7. Stir in the oats and combine mixture then remove from heat and allow it to cool for about 10 minutes.

8. Serve this special meal to your cat when you desire and store the leftovers in the fridge in a sealed air-tight container.

Chicken & Broccoli Stew

This is a healthy and filling dish that your furry friend will enjoy that is easy to prepare.

Preparation time: 10 minutes

Total Cooking time: 40 minutes

Servings: 6-8

Ingredients:

- 1,200 mg salmon oil
- ½ teaspoon calcium supplement
- 4 grams unflavored gelatin
- 1-ounce broccoli, chopped
- 1 ½ cups water
- 80 grams chicken liver, cooked and chopped
- 2 pounds chicken breast, skinless and boneless

Directions:

1. In a pan combine the chicken liver and chicken breast.

2. Add just enough water so you can cover the meat, then simmer over medium-high heat for 30 minutes, or until your chicken is cooked through.

3. In another small pan, steam the broccoli until it is tender then allow it to cool.

4. Pour the chicken liver and chicken breast liquid into a bowl and let it cool.

5. Stir in the steamed broccoli along with gelatin, salmon oil, and supplement powder.

6. Transfer into a food processor, and puree.

7. Divide the mixture into portions and chill it for about 3 hours or until the gelatin is set then serve when you desire.

Duck & Egg Recipe

This dish will have your cat doing back-flips for a bowl of it!

Preparation time: 10 minutes

Total Cooking time: 25 minutes

Servings: 1

Ingredients:

- 4.2 grams Balance IT Feline supplement
- ¼ cup frozen spinach, thawed and drained
- ¼ cup summer squash, finely diced
- 1 teaspoon canola oil
- 3 tablespoons mashed sweet potato
- ¼ cup quick-cooking oats, cooked
- 1-ounce duck breast meat
- 2 ½ large egg whites, beaten

Directions:

1. Using a skillet over medium-high heat, warm the canola oil.

2. Add the beaten egg whites to skillet, cook until set, and stir.

3. Stir in the duck meat and cook for about 20 minutes or until meat is browned.

4. Add the remaining ingredients and mix for about another 2 to 3 minutes.

5. Allow mixture to cool before serving to your cat.

Sautéed Rabbit Stew

Your cat will be rubbing around your leg when you are preparing this healthy meal for him!

Preparation time: 10 minutes

Total Cooking time: 45 minutes

Servings: 2-3

Ingredients:

- 1 cup peeled and diced carrot, sweet potato, turnip, and celery
- ¼ teaspoon dried parsley
- ¼ teaspoon dried rosemary
- ½ pound fresh rabbit meat, bone, and skin removed
- 1 teaspoon olive oil

Directions:

1. In a pan over medium-high heat, warm your olive oil.

2. Cut the rabbit meat into small bite-size chunks.

3. Add the rabbit meat to the pan and sauté until meat is browned.

4. Sprinkle the rosemary and parsley into the pan, then pour vegetable stock in the pan and stir to combine.

5. Bring your mixture to a boil, then set to simmer until the rabbit is cooked through.

6. Cook your dish over very low heat for about 45 minutes or until the vegetables are tender.

7. Allow your mixture to cool before serving it to your cat.

Chicken & Spinach Dish

This is a healthy chicken dish that will have your cat feeling content and happy!

Preparation time: 10 minutes

Total Cooking time: 20 minutes

Servings: 1-2

Ingredients:

- 3.7 grams Balance IT Feline supplement
- 2 tablespoons apple, grated
- 2 tablespoons frozen spinach, thawed
- 2 teaspoons canola oil
- 2 tablespoons brown rice, steamed
- 3 ¼ ounces chicken breast, boneless and skinless

Directions:

1. In a small pan heat the canola oil.

2. Chop the chicken into bite-size pieces and add to the pan.

3. Sauté the chicken until cooked through.

4. Add the remaining ingredients into the pan and stir to combine. Cook until warmed through.

5. Allow your mixture to cool before serving to your cat.

Chapter 2. Raw Cat Food Recipes

Raw Chicken without Bone

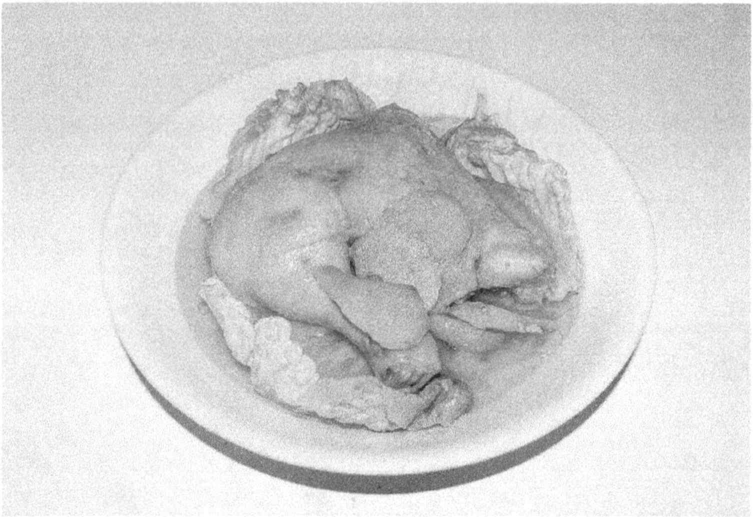

This boneless chicken meal will be a great meal to serve your loving feline friend!

Preparation time: 10 minutes

Total Cooking time: none

Servings: 6-8

Ingredients:

- 14 ounces raw chicken heart
- 3 boneless chicken thighs and drumsticks, bones removed
- 7 ounces raw chicken liver
- 800 IU vitamin E supplement
- 4,000 mg salmon oil
- 3 tablespoons bone meal
- 4 large egg yolks, whisked
- 2 cups water
- 2 tablespoons unflavored gelatin
- 4 teaspoons psyllium husk powder
- 1 ½ teaspoon light sea salt
- 200 mg vitamin B-complex supplement

Directions:

1. Remove half of the skin from chicken, then slice it into small chunks.

2. Combine the liver and heart in a small mixing bowl, then feed it through a meat grinder.

3. Add the water to mixing bowl, then whisk in the egg yolks, salmon oil, bone meal, sea salt, vitamin B-complex, and vitamin E.

4. Stir in the gelatin and psyllium husk powder, then add the organ mixture along with chopped meats.

5. Portion the cat food as desired and freeze.

Reduced-Protein Turkey Dinner

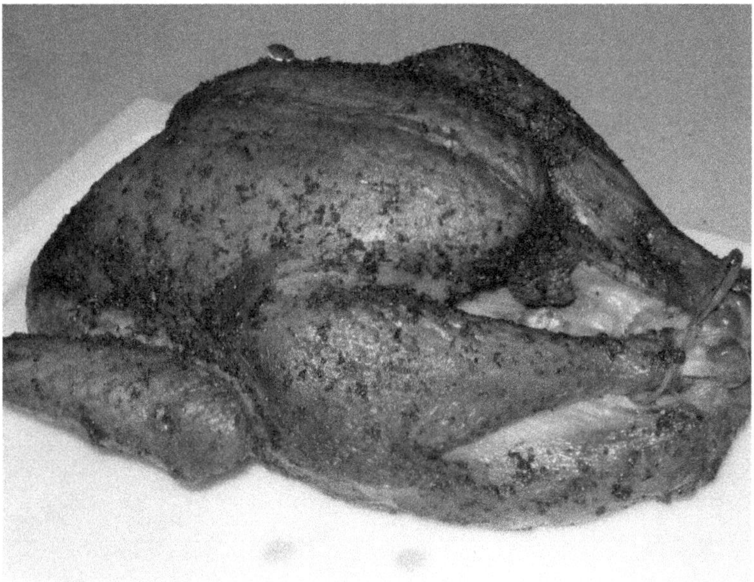

This is a cat dish that will be enjoyed by that feline that really enjoys a good turkey dinner!

Preparation time: 10 minutes

Total Cooking time: none

Servings: 4-5

Ingredients:

- 1 cup grass-fed butter, softened
- 2 cups pumpkin puree
- 200 mg vitamin B-complex supplement
- 400 IU vitamin E supplement
- 4,000 mg taurine supplement
- 4,000 mg salmon oil
- 4,500 mg calcium carbonate powder
- 2 large egg yolks, whisked
- 1 cup bottled spring water
- 2 pounds turkey breast, lean ground

Directions:

1. Add your ground turkey in a large mixing bowl.

2. In another mixing bowl, whisk eggs and water.

3. Add the taurine, calcium carbonate, vitamin E, vitamin B-complex, salmon oil, and whisk to combine.

4. Pour the liquid mixture in with the meat and stir to combine.

5. In a pan, combine the softened butter with pureed pumpkin over medium-high heat.

6. Cook the butter mixture until it has warmed through, then add in the meat mixture.

7. Toss mixture to combine well, then allow it to cool at room temperature.

8. Portion the mixture as desired then freeze.

Ground Rabbit with Bones

This is a healthy meal that will have your cat looking and feeling at his best in no time!

Preparation time: 10 minutes

Total Cooking time: none

Servings: 6-8

Ingredients:

- 8 pounds raw rabbit (organs, meat, and bone)
- 32 g Alnutrin Meat & Bone supplement
- 2 cups water

Directions:

1. Cut the rabbit into little pieces, then feed it through a meat grinder.

2. Whisk together the water and the Alnutrin supplement in a mixing bowl.

3. Pour the liquid into mixing bowl along with meat mixture and stir until well combined.

4. Portion the mixture as desired and freeze.

Turkey & Rabbit with Raw Bone

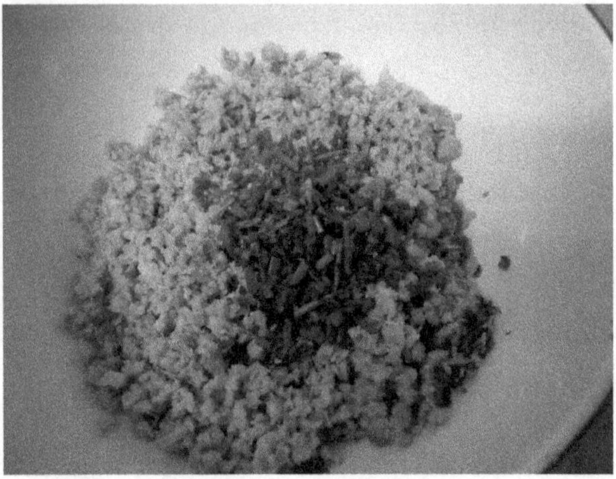

You can easily prepare this homemade dish for your feline friend that will provide them with a healthy and tasty meal that will have them licking their chops!

Preparation time: 10 minutes

Total Cooking time: none

Servings: 5-6

Ingredients:

- 200 mg vitamin B-complex supplement
- 800 IU vitamin E supplement
- 4,000 mg salmon oil
- 4 large egg yolks, whisked
- 2 cups water
- 7 ounces raw chicken or turkey liver
- 14 ounces raw chicken heart
- 2 pounds fresh rabbit meat, bones cut out and reserved
- 2 ¼ pounds fresh turkey breast, bones cut out and reserved
- 1 ½ teaspoon light sea salt
- 4 teaspoons psyllium husk powder

Directions:

1. Remove approximately half of the skin from the turkey breast and cut it into small chunks.

2. Cut the rabbit meat into bite-size pieces, keeping most of the skin on.

3. Combine the raw bones with the liver and heart in mixing bowl, then feed through a meat grinder.

4. Add the water into a mixing bowl, then whisk in the egg yolks, vitamin E, vitamin B-complex, salmon oil, and sea salt.

5. Stir in the psyllium husk powder then add in the ground bone mixture along with the chopped meats.

6. Portion the mixture as desired and freeze.

Ground Beef & Bone

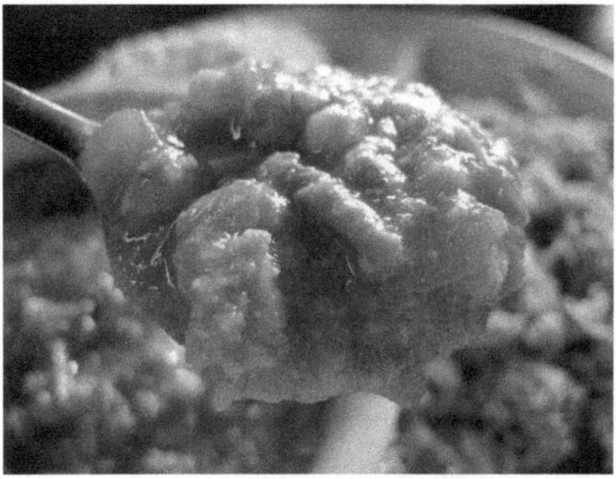

For the favorite feline that loves beef meals, this recipe is sure to get them purring with delight!

Preparation time: 10 minutes

Total Cooking time: none

Servings: 4-5

Ingredients:

- 2 large egg yolks, whisked
- ½ cup bottled spring water
- 100 grams raw chicken liver
- 100 grams raw chicken heart
- 1 ½ pounds lean ground beef, raw
- 200 mg vitamin B-complex supplement
- 400 IU vitamin E supplement
- 2,000 mg wild salmon oil
- 2,000 mg taurine supplement
- ½ teaspoon light sea salt
- 2 tablespoons ground bone meal

Directions:

1. Add the ground beef to a large mixing bowl.

2. Chop the chicken and beef hearts with the chicken livers and add to the bowl.

3. Toss the meat mixture, then feed it through the meat grinder and back into the bowl.

4. In a separate bowl, whisk the water, bone meal, and eggs.

5. Add the taurine, sea salt, salmon oil, vitamin E, vitamin B-complex, and whisk to combine mixture.

6. Add your liquid to the bowl with the ground meat and mix together.

7. Portion the mixture as desired and freeze.

Chopped Turkey & Pumpkin Dinner

Prepare this healthy tasty meal for your cat to show them that they are indeed special!

Preparation time: 10 minutes

Total Cooking time: none

Servings: 12 servings

Ingredients:

- 6 pounds turkey meat, raw, boneless
- 6.5 ounces raw turkey liver
- 2 cups organic pumpkin puree
- 2 cups water
- 40g Alnutrin with Calcium supplement

Directions:

1. Chop the turkey meat into bite-size pieces, including some skin.

2. Cut the turkey liver into small pieces and toss in mixing bowl along with turkey meat.

3. In a large mixing bowl combine the Alnutrin supplement and water.

4. Stir in the canned pumpkin, then add the turkey meat mixture.

5. Combine ingredients and mix well.

6. Portion mixture as desired and freeze.

Ground Duck Dinner

This dinner is packed with healthy goodness for your feline that will have them begging for second helpings!

Preparation time: 10 minutes

Total Cooking time: none

Servings: 6-8

Ingredients:

- 1 ½ teaspoon light sea salt
- 2,000 mg taurine supplement
- 200 IU vitamin E supplement
- 200 mg vitamin B-complex supplement
- 4,000 mg wild salmon oil
- 4 large egg yolks, whisked
- 1 cup bottled spring water
- chicken heart, chopped
- chicken liver, chopped
- 4 ½ pounds whole duck, dressed

Directions:

1. Remove half of the skin from the duck, keeping the fat, then remove 25% of the bone and chop the meat.

2. Add enough chicken liver to equal about 7 ounces and enough chicken heart to equal 14 ounces.

3. Chop the liver and heart, then add it with the chopped duck meat.

4. Feed the mixture through your meat grinder and collect it in a large mixing bowl.

5. Whisk the water and egg yolks together in a small bowl.

6. Add the salmon oil into the bowl.

7. Add the vitamin B-complex and vitamin E into a bowl and whisk to combine.

8. Whisk in the salt and taurine then add to meat mixture.

9. Portion the cat meat mixture as desired and freeze.

Chopped Chicken & Vegetable Recipe

This easy to prepare meal will have your furry friend feeling and looking energized and healthy!

Preparation time: 10 minutes

Total Cooking time: 10 minutes

Servings: 8-10

Ingredients:

- 40 g Alnutrin with Calcium supplement
- 2 cups water
- 4 large egg yolks
- ½ cup frozen peas, thawed
- 1 small carrot, peeled, chopped or grated
- 15 ounces raw chicken livers
- 15 ounces raw chicken hearts
- 4 ½ pounds chicken thighs

Directions:

1. Remove the bones and most of the skin from the chicken thighs.

2. Chop the chicken thigh meat into bite-size pieces.

3. Cut the chicken livers and hearts and toss the pieces with thigh meat in mixing bowl.

4. Cook the green peas and carrots for about 10 minutes or until they are very tender. Once cooked add them in with meat mixture along with egg yolks.

5. In another bowl mix the Alnutrin and water together.

6. Pour liquid over meat and vegetable mixture and toss to combine.

7. Portion cat food as desired and freeze.

Ground Chicken & Eggs Meal

Your cat will be purring with satisfaction after he has finished this tasty, healthy meal!

Preparation time: 10 minutes

Total Cooking time: none

Servings: 6-8

Ingredients:

- 1 tablespoon psyllium husk powder
- 1 ½ teaspoon light sea salt
- 2,000 mg taurine supplement
- 200 IU vitamin E supplement
- 200 mg vitamin B-complex supplement
- 4,000 mg wild salmon oil
- 4 large egg yolks, whisked
- 1 cup bottled spring water
- 14 ounces raw chicken heart, chopped
- 7 ounces raw chicken livers, chopped
- 4 ½ pounds chicken thighs with skin and bone

Directions:

1. Remove the skin from half of the chicken and keep the fat.

2. Slice out about 25% of the bone from the chicken thighs and cut into pieces.

3. Chop the chicken heart and liver into pieces and toss in a bowl with chicken thigh meat.

4. Feed the mixture through your meat grinder and collect in a large mixing bowl.

5. Whisk the water and egg yolks in another bowl.

6. Add salmon oil (if in capsules pierce them) then add oil into the bowl.

7. Open vitamin capsules and add contents into the bowl.

8. Whisk the sea salt and taurine in with liquid mixture, then add with meat mixture and stir.

9. Sprinkle the psyllium husk powder into the bowl and stir to combine.

10. Portion the cat food mixture as desired and freeze.

Simple Raw Chicken Dinner

This will be a favorite dinner for the feline that loves chicken!

Preparation time: 10 minutes

Total Cooking time: none

Servings: 8-12

Ingredients:

- 40 g Alnutrin with Calcium supplement
- 2 cups water
- 7 ½ ounces raw chicken liver
- 6 pounds raw chicken breasts and thighs

Directions:

1. In a mixing bowl, add chopped chicken meat along with chopped chicken liver.

2. Feed the chicken meat mixture through your meat grinder to create a uniform texture.

3. In a mixing bowl, whisk together the Alnutrin supplement and water until well combined.

4. Pour the mixture over the ground chicken meat and toss to combine.

5. Portion the cat food mixture as desired and freeze.

Chapter 3. Homemade Cat Treat Recipes

Canned Food Cookies

These are a healthy tasty treat to give your cat that is easy to prepare but will please your cat to no end!

Preparation time: 10 minutes

Total Cooking time: 30 minutes

Servings: 12 cookies

Ingredients:

- 1 can paté cat food

Directions:

1. Use a piece of parchment paper to line a baking sheet, then preheat your oven to 350° Fahrenheit.

2. Put the contents of cat food can onto a plate.

3. Cut the cat food into 1/4-inch slices then cut the slices into quarters.

4. Shape the pieces into round cookies, then place them onto a prepared baking sheet.

5. Bake your dish for approximately 30 minutes, or until the cookies are dried and crispy.

6. Cool your cookies completely, then store them in an air-tight container.

Baked Liver Bites

This recipe of liver treats will have your feline licking his chops after enjoying one!

Preparation time: 10 minutes

Total Cooking time: 12 minutes

Servings: dozen

Ingredients:

- 1 ¼ cups whole-wheat flour
- ¼ cup warm water
- ½ cup chicken livers, chopped and cooked
- 1 tablespoon coconut oil
- ¼ cup mashed sweet potato, cooked

Directions:

1. Preheat oven to 325° Fahrenheit, then line a baking sheet with foil or parchment paper.

2. Place the cooked chicken liver into a blender with water and blend until puréed.

3. In a mixing bowl, combine the whole-wheat flour and coconut oil.

4. Stir in the mashed sweet potato and blended liver.

5. Knead your mixture into a ball then roll it out to about ¼-inch thickness.

6. Slice the dough into small bite-size treats and place them on the prepared baking sheet.

7. Bake the treats for about 12 minutes or until crisp and dried.

8. Store the treats in an air-tight container in the fridge.

Cheesy Kitty Treats

If your cat has a fondness for cheese, then they will love these easy to prepare cheesy treats!

Preparation time: 10 minutes

Total Cooking time: 25 minutes

Servings: dozen

Ingredients:

- ¼ cup yellow cornmeal
- ¾ cup whole-wheat flour
- ¼ cup plain Greek yogurt, non-fat
- ¼ cup Parmesan cheese, grated
- ¾ cup cheddar cheese, shredded

Directions:

1. Preheat your oven to 350° Fahrenheit, then line a baking sheet with parchment paper.

2. In a mixing bowl combine yogurt and cheese.

3. Add the cornmeal and whole-wheat flour and stir into a dough.

4. If you need to add a bit of water to the dough so that it sticks together then roll it into a ball.

5. Roll the dough out to ¼-inch thick and cut into bite-size pieces.

6. Place the treats onto the prepared baking sheet and bake for 25 minutes or until treats are crisp and dried.

7. Cool treats completely and then store them in an air-tight container.

Tasty Tuna Tidbits

What cat would not love these tasty tuna treats? I am sure your cat will come running when you take these treats out!

Preparation time: 10 minutes

Total Cooking time: 20 minutes

Servings: dozen

Ingredients:

- ¼ cup yellow cornmeal
- ½ cup whole-wheat flour
- ¼ cup water
- 1 large egg white, cooked and chopped
- 1 (6-ounce) can of tuna stored in water, drained

Directions:

1. Preheat the oven to 350° Fahrenheit and line a baking sheet with parchment paper.

2. In a mixing bowl, flake the tuna and stir in the egg white with water.

3. Stir in the cornmeal and whole-wheat flour until it forms a dough.

4. Knead the dough into a ball then roll it out into a 1/4-inch thickness.

5. Cut the dough into bite-size pieces and place them on the prepared baking sheet.

6. Bake for 20 minutes or until dried and crisp.

7. Store your cat treats in an air-tight container in the fridge.

Chicken Biscuits

Your cat is sure to love these yummy kitty chicken biscuits that are easy to prepare!

Preparation time: 10 minutes

Total Cooking time: 20 minutes

Servings: dozen

Ingredients:

- ¼ cup yellow cornmeal
- 1 cup whole-wheat flour
- ½ cup chicken broth, low-sodium
- 1 ½ cups cooked chicken breast, shredded, boneless, skinless
- 1 tablespoon of coconut oil

Directions:

1. Preheat your oven to 350° Fahrenheit and line a baking sheet with a parchment paper.

2. Mix the chicken meat and chicken broth with coconut oil in a food processor.

3. Pulse the ingredients several times to combine well.

4. Add the cornmeal, and whole-wheat flour then pulse until a dough is formed.

5. Roll your dough into a ball, then roll it out to 1/4-inch thickness.

6. Slice the dough into bite-size pieces and place on prepared baking sheet.

7. Bake your cat treat for 20 minutes or until crisp and dried.

8. Cool treats completely and store them in an air-tight container.

Beefy Bites

Your cat will love these beefy treats and will come running when they see you taking them out!

Preparation time: 10 minutes

Total Cooking time: 8 minutes

Servings: dozen

Ingredients:

- 3 small jars beef baby food
- 1 tablespoon water or canned tuna liquid
- 1 ½ cups wheat germ

Directions:

1. Combine all of your ingredients in a mixing bowl.

2. Cover a plate with a piece of parchment paper.

3. Spoon the cat treat mixture onto the plate in rounded ¼ teaspoons.

4. Cook the treats in the microwave for 8 minutes on high or until they are firm.

5. Store your cat treats in an air-tight container and keep it in the fridge.

Conclusion

I hope that you and your feline friend will both enjoy and benefit from preparing this collection of wonderful healthy homemade cat meals and treats for many years to come. I can assure you that I know you are going to feel much more confident and certain of what exactly is going into your cat's foods because you will be in total control of this! You will not only be providing your feline friend with good quality meals and treats, but you will also gain a sense of contentment. This you will gain in knowing that you are doing your best to make sure that the meals you provide for your pet are not only healthy but are going to be enjoyed entirely by them right down to the last morsel!

Author's Afterthoughts

Thanks ever so much to each of my cherished readers for investing the time to read this book!

I know you could have picked from many other books but you chose this one. So a big thanks for downloading this book and reading all the way to the end.

If you enjoyed this book or received value from it, I'd like to ask you for a favor. Please take a few minutes to post an honest and heartfelt review on Amazon.com. Your support does make a difference and helps to benefit other people.

Thanks for your Reviews!

Rachael Rayner

About the Author

Rachael Rayner

Are you tired of cooking the same types of dishes over and over again? As a mother of not one, but two sets of twins, preparing meals became very challenging, very early on. Not only was it difficult to get enough time in the kitchen to prepare anything other than fried eggs, but I was constantly trying to please 4 little hungry mouths under 5 years old. Of course I would not trade my angels for anything in the world, but I had just about given up on cooking, when I had a genius idea one afternoon while I was napping beside one of my sons. I am so happy and proud to tell you that since then, my kitchen has become my sanctuary and my children have become my helpers. I have transformed my meal preparation, my grocery shopping habits, and my cooking style. I am Racheal Rayner, and I am proud to tell you that I am no longer the boring mom sous-chef people avoid. I am the house in our neighborhood where every kid (and parent) wants to come for dinner.

I was raised Jewish in a very traditional household, and I was not allowed in the kitchen that much. My mother cooked the same recipes day in day out, and salt and pepper were probably the extent of the seasonings we were able to detect in the dishes she made. We did not even know any better until we moved out of the house. My husband, Frank is a foodie. I thought I was too, until I met him. I mean I love food, but who doesn't right? He revolutionized my knowledge about cooking. He used to take over in the kitchen, because after all, we were a modern couple and both of us worked full time jobs. He prepared chilies, soups, chicken casseroles—one more delicious than the last. When I got pregnant with my first set of twins and had to stay home on bed rest, I took over the kitchen and it was a disaster. I tried so hard to find the right ingredients and recipes to make the dishes taste something close to my husband's. However,

I hated follow recipes. You don't tell a pregnant woman that her food tastes bad, so Frank and I reluctantly ate the dishes I prepared on week days. Fortunately, he was the weekend chef.

After the birth of my first set of twins, I was too busy to even attempt to cook. Sure, I prepared thousands of bottles of milk and purees, but Frank and I ended up eating take out 4 days out of 5. Then, no break for this mom, I gave birth to my second set of twins only 19 months later! I knew that now it was not just about Frank and I anymore, but it was about these little ones for whom I wanted to cook healthy meals, and I had to learn how to cook.

One afternoon in March, when I got up from that power nap with my boys, I had figured out what I needed to do to improve my cooking skills and stop torturing my family with my bland dishes. I had to let go of everything I had learned, tasted, or seen from my childhood and start over. I spent a week organizing my kitchen, and I equipped myself a new blender. I also got some fun shaped cookie cutters, a rolling pin, wooden spatulas, mixing bowls, fruit cutters, and plenty of plastic storage containers. I was ready.

My oldest twins, Isabella and Sophia are now teenagers, and love to cook with their Mom when they are not too busy talking on the phone. My youngest twins Erick and John, are now 10 years old and so helpful in the kitchen, especially when it's time to make cookies.

Let me start sharing my tips, recipes, and shopping suggestions with you ladies and gentlemen. I did not reinvent the wheel here but I did make my kitchen my own, started storing my favorite baking ingredients, and visiting the fresh produce market more often. I have mastered the principles of slow cooking and chopping veggies ahead of time. I have even embraced the involvement of my little ones in the kitchen with me.

I never want to hear you say that you are too busy to cook some delicious and healthy dishes, because BUSY, is my middle name.

www.ingramcontent.com/pod-product-compliance
Lightning Source LLC
LaVergne TN
LVHW091942210126
830210LV00008B/252

* 9 7 8 1 6 9 1 1 5 7 2 7 3 *